In the Cold of the Sun

Children in Crisis
poems and narratives

by Johnnye Jo Lott

FIELDS PUBLISHING INC.
NASHVILLE, TENNESSEE

Published by

FIELDS
PUBLISHING

Fields Publishing Inc.
917 Harpeth Valley Place • Nashville, Tennessee 37221
615-662-1344
e-mail: tfields@fieldspublishing.com

Contents

Foreword

One fact that becomes more evident to me as each year passes is that childhood is not always the carefree, happy-go-lucky time that it is often characterized to be. Almost every day the news media report at least one story of a child who was abused or even killed at the hands of an adult or another child. In the wake of the tragedy of September 11, 2001, we read of children who have faced the agonizing loss of parents or other relatives to the terrorist attacks on America. These stories affront our sensitivities as almost nothing else can.

I grieve for these children and for countless others born into poverty and other circumstances not of their making. I feel a strange mixture of sadness and pride in disabled children or children with differences who must deal with major odds each day of their lives and yet must face a world that is often uninformed and brutal.

The poems in this book are about those children. They are an expression of outrage and grief, but also a tribute to the wonderful spirit of these youngsters. I have known them all—as you have—in our families, in our classrooms, in our synagogues and churches, and in our cities.

I dedicate these poems to the children and to those of you who know and love them.

Johnnye Jo Lott
Murfreesboro, NC
2002

Seeking a New September

The effects of the September 11, 2001, attack on our beloved America reached around the world. Millions of people were directly or indirectly affected. That day in September forever changed the lives of the families of those killed by terrorists in the terrible events that occurred. More than a thousand children lost parents, including several hundred who lost the only parent they had ever known. Many newly-single parents, while dealing with their own losses, were thrust into the unfamiliar role of sole caretaker, and many children had to adjust to new situations that further compounded the upset and grief they experienced.

But the human spirit is strong, and there is hope of healing and new beginnings in a new September.

Seeking a New September

The mother is presumed dead,
Among the missing at Ground Zero.
Her picture, soiled now
With the salt of fingers and lips,
Seems to be fading,
Retreating from the man's outstretched hand
As if to attest to her leaving.

The room and the television set are dark,
The room dimmed by shadows
Of late afternoon and heavy hearts;
The television has been silenced from the news,
But smoky images seared on his mind
Roil in constant replay
As if on every wall.

The boy he hugs to his chest
Lies in fitful sleep,
Both comfort and enigma,
Forcing on the man a charge
He feels too raw to ponder.
He clings to the child
As if to suck from him
Some unnatural strength
That will help him
To take her place.

Assurances come hard
From a chasm of fear,
And loss leaves holes
That can't be filled
Like graves, with dirt.
Hurt sends deep roots
Into a young and fertile mind.
The father's pain is entwined
With the boy's—and even a nation's.
A wife and a mother died,
And a nation was torn
From the breast of its motherland.

He pulls the child closer,
Knowing that even such grief knows limits;
And life will again
Be illumined by good.
He knows that, in time,
August days will melt
Into another September
With its golden promises
Of new beginnings;
And he, the child, and a nation
Will rise from the ashes
And claim them again.

—January, 2002

Deena, African Queen

As a teacher in a small Georgia town in the 70s, I was inspired and humbled by the dignity and pride with which many impoverished children dealt with their lots in life. They often teased and sparred with each other, as if to relieve the tension of their own wretched existence. Yet I witnessed and experienced an unexpected gentleness and joy that seemed to emanate from within and manifest itself on their faces. Deena, an improbable "African Queen," was one of my favorite gentle students.

Deena, African Queen

Head held high as an African Queen
    She glides through the door
    In her pinned-up dress
    And sole-slapping shoes.

Black, kinky-wire hair
    In corkscrew braids
    Flecked with white fuzz
    Clings to her head like a bur.

The scent of wood stove smoke
    Trails in the air as she passes
    Grinning classmates
    Aching for a fight.

She tosses them a wilting,
    Eye-corner glance,
    Daring and defying
    Their taunts,

Plops self and books
    Into the desk,
    And turns a gentle smile
    On her teacher;

Enigmatic royalty,
    Awaiting the feast of the day.

—1998

Laws of the Heart

Far too many children experience physical and emotional abuse at the hands of parents or guardians. Often, those most in a position to help them–teachers, social workers, or childcare providers—dread and avoid becoming involved. As a result, numerous children suffer heart–breaking and sometimes life-threatening punishment from the ones whom they should be able to trust the most.

Laws of the Heart

She came to me in the early spring,
This proud-pariah-of-a-girl,
Flipping her oily hair in defiance
When they teased her about the blouse.
"I'm just cold-natured," she'd say,
Although it was eighty in the shade.
I knew, though I didn't want to,
That it hid the livid mark on her arm
But couldn't hide the fading bruise by her mouth.

I didn't want to ask
Why she missed school so much,
Only to appear again one day
With fatigue in her shoulders
And no response in her eyes.
I just couldn't take knowing,
Even when she'd cling to me at recess
Like hair on a sweater,
Hinting at lurid stories from home.
"We slept in the car last night," she'd say,
And I'd smile and change the subject.
Then I'd catch her out of the corner of my eye
Jabbing holes with her pencil
In a picture she'd drawn,
And later I'd find in the trash can
The wadded drawing of a man.

It was almost May
When she missed school for two weeks,
And I thought she'd moved on.

I was breathing a little easier
But not sleeping well at night.
Then one day she just showed up,
Wearing the same blouse
And a fresh bruise by her eye.
And suddenly I wanted to know.
Taking her by the hand,
I led her to the school office,
Following the laws of the land
And the laws of the heart.

—1998

In the Cold of the Sun

The divorce of parents often takes a toll on children that may go unnoticed by the adults caught up in their own problems and grief. Even when divorce seems to be the only solution, fear, uncertainty, and self-blame are common byproducts of a broken home.

In the Cold of the Sun

She doesn't see or feel the sun
Where she sits near the window
Huddled in the shabby sweat shirt
He'd worn every evening for as long
As she could recall
When he would stretch out
On his old easy chair
In retreat from the day.

She fingers the photograph
In a tarnished frame
Dabs at a tear traveling
Down her cheek.
Smiling faces blur
Through the glass.
She pulls the shirt close
Against the cold of the sun.

Once his love for them
Seemed real to her;
Now she knows that he longed to leave,
That maybe it wasn't that at all.
The bitter muffled words
She'd heard them speak
Behind closed doors
Fill her mind yet
Like thunder's deafening roar
And buffet her heart with fear.
She shivers in the sun.

In their grief and sickening rage
They do not know that she heard
And blames herself
For the rift that leaves
Their world so cold.
But if they did,
Would they have tried
To sing a different song,
To walk a different road?

–1998

Child of Sorrow and Blessing

I watched firsthand the sorrows—and the blessings—of a situation in which a beautiful child was born out of wedlock into a respectable and loving family. The young parents had made a mistake, but they felt that a marriage that neither of them wanted would only compound their problem. Although out-of-wedlock births are more accepted now than in earlier days, the trauma of such an event is often real and devastating for families with traditional values who live in more conservative surroundings. I observed with joy and amazement how the tiny blonde girl born into that family wrapped herself around the lives of staid and prudish adults, never once aware that she might not be entitled to life on equal terms.

Child of Sorrow and Blessing

Little girl with golden hair falling free around your face
wearing your smile like well-worn jeans
not dreaming of the pain you brought.
Innocent bearer of agony.

Wee child born of his sorrow and hers
wrapping your life around their hearts;
laughing and singing your childhood songs.
Tiny dove on a mission of peace.

If God but wills you'll never know
how they dreaded your presence here
until you blessed their lives with love.
Precious bearer of harmony.

Lives have changed because you came
though grief lurks 'round your door.
May God protect you in this world,
guiltless child of love.

—1997

Round Man

Few forms of child abuse are more prevalent than that endured by overweight children at the hands of their peers and unthinking adults who care for them on a regular basis. Teasing, bullying and humiliation are the daily fare for many children who do not fit the stereotypical image of normal size or appearance. The flip treatment of this problem and the attitude that fat should be punished has driven too many young people to the brink of despair—and sometimes even over the edge.

Round Man

We never were sure about his real name;
    Jonathan, we thought;
    Just called 'im "Round Man"—
    Suited 'im better,
    Big guy for just fifteen;
    Could've been a good lineman for the team,
    But his big belly made 'im too slow.

God, he was a million laughs;
    Coach would make 'im run laps
    When he caught 'im with a Hershey or somethin'.
    We'd cheer and clap,
    And he'd huff 'n puff 'round the field,
    Sweatin' like a hog.
    He'd laugh, too, and raise both fists
    Like an Olympic champ.

Once we saw 'im cry,
    And Coach said he was bringin' it on himself,
    Eatin' so much junk;
    And he wouldn't eat anything in front of us for awhile;
    And we'd tease 'im with our candy bars
    Until he'd cave in and eat three or four
    Just for the hell of it.

Once in class, when he bent over to pick up a pencil,
    His pants ripped up the back,
    And we all broke up—
    The teacher, too—
    And Round Man just did a funny little jig
    And laughed louder than anybody.

That's the thing I don't understand;
    He was always happy—
    Class clown,
    Makin' jokes about his fat,
    Puffin' out his cheeks and stomach
    To show how fat he could really be;
    And he'd even laugh when
    The older guys on the team
    Punched 'im and called 'im names.

The girls gave 'im a hard time, too.
    They laughed behind his back
    At how his belly lapped over his pants;
    And on a dare
    He asked a cheerleader for a date—
    With all of us watchin'—
    Just to see her friends squeal and giggle
    While she stammered and blushed.
    He really was a million laughs.

But even though he seemed smart,
    He couldn't make good grades.
    Once his mama came up to school—
    She was big 'n fat, too—
    So I guess he got it natural—
    And a girl that works in the office
    Overheard some talk
    About somebody pickin' on Round Man
    (Jonathan, his mama called 'im)
    And about cryin' at night
    And not bein' able to study;

And then Mr. Allen, the principal,
    Tellin' her until he got his weight down
    Kids were just goin' to say those things,
    So he might as well get used to it,
    And maybe she should
    Encourage 'im not to eat so much;
    And besides, Jonathan
    (Mr. Allen usually called him Round Man, too)
    Never showed he was upset at school;
    He was always laughin' and askin' for it;
    But he'd see what he could do.

I kinda liked Round Man, myself;
    He never said mean things to people;
    And I remember in the third grade
    When I wet my pants on accident,
    He was about the only one in class who didn't laugh at me;
    And he volunteered to go with me to the nurse.

He could really play the trumpet good,
    But he couldn't march in the band
    Because they didn't have a uniform
    Big enough.
    That didn't bother Round Man, either;
    He just laughed and said,
    "Good—I won't have to practice so much."

That's just the way he was—
    Jolly all the time,
    Like all fat people;
    So how could he do this?
    He was so happy.

        —1997

Punishing Words

For an astonishingly large number of children, school is a frustrating and heartbreaking experience. Many of these students have neurologically-caused learning disabilities, or dyslexia, that may affect their ability to read or perform any number of school tasks.

Too often they suffer self-doubt and failure in their academic work. With their "hidden disabilities," they may become targets of ridicule from their classmates, who view them as incompetent or lazy.

Parents and teachers are frequently puzzled and dismayed when bright and talented students are unable to learn to read, write or perform math. They are saddened—and sometimes angered—as they watch personal and behavioral problems unfold in a child who is trying to compensate for his or her lack of success in school.

But some parents can look back on their own young years and remember and understand—all too well.

Punishing Words

The man is well-acquainted
with his son's tears
over pages splashed
with punishing words
parading in drunken lines
reeling, falling,
marching in reverse.

The boy, hunched over the book
in sullen determination
reminds him of long-ago
spirit-bruising days
when school felt
more molesting
than educating;

When despair
transformed him
into a preposterous clown
acting out his humiliation
for classmates
he longed to persuade
of his worth.

His son had told him
of the names they called him
to show their scorn—
names familiar and wounding
that the father wears yet
in the pit of his heart.

He wants to tell the boy
that reading isn't all of life,
but for now he knows it is.

—1998

No Wednesday's Child

Attention-deficit hyperactivity disorder (ADHD) can be a devastating crisis in the life of a child. Due to the underachievement and sometimes impulsive and out-of-control behavior that is typical of youngsters who suffer this malady, bright and innocent children are often subjected to threats, punishment and dire predictions by parents and teachers who do not understand the disorder. Words spoken by frustrated adults to a child already puzzled and disconcerted by his inability to control his life and actions can crush the spirit and cause irreparable damage to self-esteem.

Science is making strides in the understanding of ADHD and, with proper treatment, many children and adults, alike, have been blessed with life again. The poem, No Wednesday's Child, is the story of one young boy, born with a high IQ, but hindered in numerous ways by attention deficit hyperactivity disorder that was diagnosed only after he became an adult.

No Wednesday's Child

He arrived in the world running,
    always in a hurry, always in a jam;
    now darting across my mind
    wiry and blonde
    with freckles on his nose
    and mischief in his eyes.

Spunky four-year-old whirlwind
    on his way to the next calamity,
    doling out hugs
    and precocious alibis.

At school he dazzled
    with his needle-sharp mind,
    devouring words like a ravenous pup;
    but the words turned into paradox,
    exciting, elating,
    perplexing and punishing:

Enthusiastic—impulsive,
Witty—class clown
Gifted—underachiever,
Talented—unmotivated,
Creative—disorganized,
Attentive—distracted.

Good intentions
    in a tug-of-war
    with the reality
    in his head.

High school grades and life yo-yoed;
    he was headed toward grief,
    surrounded by inadvertent abusers,
    accusing, cajoling,
    warning of disaster,
    driving him
    into
    despair.

In college he outran the demons
    crouching in his mind;
    he was on the road to the future,
    lugging a load too heavy
    for his weary shoulders.

But science and courage
    would lift him up,
    for he was
    no Wednesday's Child.

Diagnosis and treatment
    fell as rain on the desert—
    a gift for the living of life.

In my mind I see him again:
    young man, still eager and restless,
    but a lilt in his step,
    faded freckles on his nose,
    and mischief in his eyes.

—1997

A Promise

One day, when I was volunteering in a first-grade class, a beautiful little girl named Kaley sidled up to me shyly and said, "I was student of the week one time." I acted impressed and chatted briefly.

At the end of the class, she broke from the lunch line and approached me again. "I was student of the week in kindergarten, too," she offered expectantly.

"That is something to be very proud of, Kaley, " I replied, and she returned to her line at the door.

When I was recounting the exchange to her teacher later, she informed me that Kaley's mother had abandoned her recently, leaving her in the care of her divorced grandfather. I knew then that this precious child had sought me out—a complete stranger—trying to fill a need deeper than I could even comprehend.

"Can you imagine," asked her teacher, "being six years old and not even knowing where your mother is?"

A Promise

He cradles the coffee mug
Forcing his gaze out the window
Away from the girl,
Daughter of his daughter.

She stirs the cereal,
Prolonging the moment,
Finally takes one flake into her spoon,
Lifts it to her lips,
Dripping milk on Piglet and Pooh
Adorning the bib of her overalls.

She drops the spoon into the bowl,
Announces that she's through.
He doesn't argue;
"It's time for the bus," he says.
She takes the lunch kit from his hand;
"I put in two cookies today," he says, anxious.
It doesn't register on her face.

His mind, rusty, unaccustomed,
Inventories the child:
Hair brushed, shoelaces tied,
Book bag and milk money in hand;
He wipes her mouth with a wet cloth;
The milk ring goes, the sadness stays.

He holds her to him, longer than usual,
Embracing his own child through her;
"I want to stay with you," she says, clinging to him;
"I'll be here when you get back," he answers;
"It's a promise."
"Will she be here?"
Cautious hope in her voice;
"Maybe," he says, knowing better.

He watches her trudge to the bus.
"I'm an old man,"
He whispers to her back,
"But I'll by-god be here
When you get back."

—1998

A Promise:
The Epilogue

Kaley's mother surfaced much later than the events referred to in the poem, "A Promise." As it turns out, she was in jail on a narcotics conviction and is presently trying to put her life back together in a halfway house. Kaley is eight years old now. Her mother is still unable to care for her.

Her beloved grandfather—the only stable person in Kaley's life—died this past winter. The loving first-grade teacher told me that she asked to keep the little girl with her during the days surrounding the funeral so that she could have a comforting environment in which to grieve and to process her loss. Kaley broke her teacher's heart when she looked up into her face and said, "I don't know what they're going to do with me now."

A Promise: The Epilogue

At the funeral home, before the others came,
    I watched from another room,
    allowing her this last private visit with him.
Humming in short bursts of sound,
    as if to defy the silence,
    she faced the casket,
    incongruous in its beauty.
With one finger she traced the satin gathers,
    rubbed her cheek against them,
    and pinched off a bloom
    trailing over the side,
    crushing it in her fist.

At last, on tiptoe, she peered in at him,
    her grandfather,
    her Pa-Pa,
    her beloved bulwark.
Unexpectedly she smiled,
    put a finger to her lips
    and shushed an imaginary visitor;
"Listen to him snore," I saw, more than heard, her say.
With outstretched fingers
    she tickled the lifeless chin,
    showered his face with the broken petals from her hand,
    and ducked beneath the casket
    in playful, hopeful laughter.

Then, in surrender to the truth,
    She rose to his side again, patted his hand,
    And her lips formed their last expectant plea:
"Pa-Pa? Pa-Pa? You promised."

From where I stood,
    I watched her head drop
    and rest on the coffin's edge.
I breathed a prayer
    against
        her unspeakable loss.

               —2000

A Freedom Denied

A large number of American children are forced by circumstance to spend long and exhausting hours in the labor force of this country. They work all day in fields, orchards, factories, and construction sites, and then, more often than not, go home at night to a life of poverty and deprivation. Even though federal laws exist to prevent this situation, companies and individual employers continue to violate the law for their own benefit.

Americans who love their country are deeply offended by those who desecrate the freedoms it affords—perhaps especially those of its youngest and most vulnerable citizens. Meanwhile, these American children are deprived of their childhood as they live on damaged dreams.

Note: Background information and ideas for this poem come from an Associated Press article entitled "Child Labor: The Voices," by Verena Dobnik and Ted Anthony, which appeared in The Virginian Pilot *on December 15, 1997.*

The lyrics of the song, "My Country, 'Tis of Thee," were written by Samuel F. Smith, 1808-1895.

A Freedom Denied

My country, 'tis of thee,
    In America's enchanted land of the West,
    A tiny girl squats on scrawny knees,
    Picking peppers in the morning chill,
    Waiting only for the sun;
    Her brother, lugging giant pails of chilies
    Trembles under the load,
    Dreaming futile childhood dreams,
    And their mother, a row away,
    Bends her back and wipes away a tear.

Sweet Land of Liberty—of thee I sing!
    In the thriving North, in another state,
    A slender girl with too few years
    Trims threads from a coat she longs to own,
    While at her feet rats scuttle across filthy factory floors
    As sewing machines drum out their dirge of despair.

Land where my fathers died...
    In a field way down in the sunny South,
    A six-year-old with almond eyes and elfin hands
    Wipes away the sweat and pulls her beans one by one,
    Creating her own private game
    And willing the day to end
    When she will fall into bed,
    Too exhausted and too sad to dream anymore.

Land of the Pilgrim's pride...
    All across the U.S.A,
    Fledgling factory hands, working too long for illegal pay;
    Youthful construction workers—
    Beardless builders of buildings—lacking foundations of
       their own;
    Young fruit pickers in fruitless tasks, dreaming of another
       world;
    Mushroom pickers in windowless huts, living out their
       puberty in the dark;
    Callow babes, too soon adults, living lives not fit for
       thieves.

From every mountainside,

Let freedom ring!

—1998

Behind the Face

Children who bear scars or disfigurement of any type often find themselves the object of ridicule or rude curiosity from insensitive children and even adults. Going to school or into the public anywhere can become a test of spirit and courage. They learn quickly how much value is put upon physical appearance in our society, and they learn just as rapidly that they do not measure up. Irreparable damage can assault the self-esteem of these youngsters.

The inspiration for this poem derives from the experiences described by Lucy Grealy in her beautiful and heartbreaking book, *Autobiography of a Face* (1994, Houghton Mifflin Company, New York).

Behind the Face

After the cancer,
    the year she was twelve,
She avoided mirrors –
    or found a way to look right through them,
Away from the damaged face
    and the chemo-baldness
Covered poorly by a hat.

But she couldn't escape the reflection
    in the eyes of the giggling, taunting schoolboys
Who called her "Baldy" or told her
    to take off her mask
And then doubled over in sickening glee.

She pretended not to hear
    and hoped to outlast her fear,
But each new meeting
    brought new dread
Of averted glances,
    repulsion or pity in their eyes—
Pity she hated
    even more than the hostility.
She took to sidling down the school halls,
    face turned to the floor,
Hiding out when she could,
    and feeling lonely and ugly.
She even wondered if maybe they had a right
    to make fun of someone so horrid.

She wanted to hate them,
    but she tried to forgive.
In time she learned well
    how to hate instead
The girl behind the face.

—1998

Cold War

A familiar story for many families is that in which a rebellious child, or a child who for no obvious reason, begins to fail or to do poorly in school and to flout the traditional values of the family. While parents experience grief, frustration, and anger over this turn of events, the child may be masking problems of his own identity and self-concept with studied bravado, laziness or defiance. Regardless of the cause, which in many cases goes undiagnosed, the effects on family relationships are akin to a war in which two opposing camps have been firmly established.

Cold War

The cigarette has left him nauseous
Its acrid taste lingering like a strange balm
Masking his injured pride.
He waves his grade card aloft
For the pubescent crowd
In a spurious show of derring-do,
Flaunting his failure in unconvincing glee.
He mocks the teacher in whining voice,
High-fives a friend,
Flicks the cigarette butt to the street.

On the walk home he tries to remember
When playground turned to battleground
And he armed himself against them.
He only knows that now
They speak in anger, a different tongue.
His mother wears a worried frown
That he has learned to avoid and despise.
His father, who used to carry him shoulder-high,
Tramples him now with tones of scorn;
Trust and pride have turned to shame and doubt.
He wounds them by acts that turn back on him;
He speaks a language they do not know.

Sometimes in regret
He longs for ice-cream party days

Of joy and celebration of jobs well-done;
For shared pride
And the journey traveled hand-in-hand.
But now he sails an untried route
Toward his future,
Casting off his mental gifts
Like extra cargo on a sinking ship.

He slowly ascends the front steps,
Shakes his long hair into his eyes,
Slumps his shoulders into his untucked shirt,
Reaches for the doorknob,
The grade card, like a trusted weapon,
Clutched tight in his sweaty hands,
And walks into battle.

—1999

Search for the Pearl

Some children reach adulthood never having realized their talents and aspirations. Despite the possibilities others see in them, they may live for a long time, floundering and uncertain, and even enduring hardships, before they discover the gifts that will lead them to their dreams.

Search for the Pearl

Though he wears a shock of gray
Where dark locks once fell
And furrows lie
Over clear blue eyes,
A boy still lives inside,
Adrift and undefined,
Always auditioning for his role in life,
Sometimes turning his back on himself.

His gifts languish
As they did on Christmases long ago
When he cast them aside
To play with the boxes.
When did he lose the scent
On the trail to his dreams?
Will he follow with his heart
The next diverging road
That may lead him to the pearl
That lies buried in his soul?

—1998

And a Little Child Shall Lead Them

Courage, awareness, and inspiration can arise from the most unexpected places. My own family, steeped in grief over the blindness of our grandchild, Amber, gained a whole new appreciation for the grit and raw determination of human beings to overcome the limitations of handicaps. Through her remarkable spirit and achievements, this small child led our family to a deep understanding and respect for a significant segment of our society.

And a Little Child Shall Lead Them

Tiny child born to a darkened world,
How could we know that your unseeing eyes
Would open our own so wide?
Should we have known that though you had no sight
You would have vision beyond your years?
We wept for the darkness that could not be fixed;
Perhaps we were wrong.
But how could we know that a child with a cane
Could lead a whole family to light?

—1997

Blind Solace

W ho of us has not promoted, or at least considered, the idea that a child, blind from birth, has an advantage over one who becomes blind later in life? "Well, you know," we say, "she's actually better off being blind from birth...."

I admit, with some degree of shame, that I have expressed that bit of untried wisdom. However, with painful personal experience and much introspection, I have come to know that, while blindness at any time in life is extremely difficult, blindness from birth is not an advantage.

Blind Solace

She's better off, they say,
Being blind from birth,
Never knowing
What she's missing.

Words of comfort
Delivered with care,
Meaning to console,
Miss their mark.

Just think, they reason,
If she'd had vision
And then lost it?
It's really best this way.

My heart knows better
And silently challenges
Well-meant words
Aimed at my grief.

Is she better off
Never to have seen
   ...a blue October sky
   ...a rainbow after a storm
   ...the color of spring
   ...a mountain
   ...a bird on the wing
   ...or her mother's smile?

Compassionate friends,
Blinder than the child,
Offer words of solace,
That cut to the bone.

—1997

47

Handicapped Accessible

"Handicapped accessible" is an important concept and reality for those children who are limited by disabilities. Modified facilities enable them to attend school with non-handicapped students. Too often though, children who are different because of their disabilities, face a disturbing absence of a certain accessibility that affects the heart and soul.

Handicapped Accessible

The wheelchair isn't the problem:
The lift on the special ed bus sets her down,
Chair and all, on the asphalt,
Like a big Huey in a textbook landing.

She's Tara Lipinski on ice
As she glides over the ramp
And through the wide hall
Lined with mini-skirted girls
In giggling threes and fours.

They wave a hand to her, or don't;
Adolescent boys hanging out
In blatant self-concern
Seem not to see her at all.

At the closed classroom door,
She parks near Annie and some others
Who talk of weekend plans
Of dates and spending the night
And movies and malls and invitations—
But not to her.

They lean on her chair
And don't know she's there;
"Hey, Annie," she tries to say,
But her tongue refuses to work.
Her reed-thin hands
Do a palsied dance in her lap;
She tries to still them.

The classroom door opens and
By habit they clear the way for her
To wheel to the modified desk
At the front of the room.

She thinks of the long weekend ahead,
The silent phone, the lonely hours,
And wonders why
They don't make this school
Handicapped accessible.

—1998

The Assailant

A large number of children are afraid to go to school. They avoid lunch, recess and playtimes because they fear they will be hurt or humiliated by bullies. This fear can interfere with learning and cause depression. At the expense of smaller, physically different or weaker children, bullies gain status or possessions for themselves.

The effects of bullying may remain active and destructive for years in the minds of victims and may continue even far into adulthood.

The Assailant

I was just eight
    that harrowing third-grade year
    when he rode into my life
    on a big yellow school bus.
He swaggered
    like a blustering bounty hunter
    on the trail for the spoil.

He sniffed out my fear
    and went for the kill.
Like a looming cloud
    he blocked the sun from my days,
    he assailed me with names
    and in his path my courage oozed away.

I cringed and cowered
    as he bullied and pushed.
He demanded my money
    and stole my pride.
On my trampled spirit
    he established his might.
My shame gave him joy;
    I bore the cost
    of making him proud.

Then suddenly he left
    as he came,
    taking his torment along,
    but leaving
    a well-defined scar
    on my soul.

—1998

To the Invisible Child

Although great strides have been made in laws that prohibit discrimination based on race, people of certain ethnic and racial groups still experience in their daily lives subtle, and sometimes blatant, incidents of prejudice and hate. And even though many white Americans find these deeds to be despicable, their own self-concern or a lack of courage often deters them from speaking in behalf of the oppressed.

The poem *To the Invisible Child* was written in response to an actual incident related to me by a good friend who still carries the burden of regret after many years.

To the Invisible Child

You were a child then,
Small, dark and beautiful,
A waist-high contrast in a lily-white parade
At the fast-food counter;
Eager for the taste of well-loved treats
And proud to be sent by your mother
To do a big boy's job.
I watched as the waiter behind the counter
Looked right over you time and again
To serve someone taller and whiter behind you,
I was appalled, but I said nothing—
Not even when you looked up at me
As if to ask, "Am I invisible?
Why can't he see me?"
And not even when I took my burger and fries
And left you standing there.

Tho' years have passed since that day,
Each brown-velvet face on a strong young man
Strums chords deep in me
Down where guilt and shame go to hide out.
I see you over and over again
In a thousand faces.
If you notice how I avert my eyes,
Then know that it is because
I repent
My callous neglect.

—1999

Fog on Turtle Mountain

For more than a century, which included the first few decades of the 1900's, many thousands of American Indian children endured misery and abuse at government boarding schools or church-run mission schools. There was a deliberate and often brutal effort to strip Indian children of their tribal language, religion, appearance, and culture. Matt Kelly, in an Associated Press article on abuse in mission and government boarding schools (*The Virginian Pilot*, April 30, 1999), tells of a young man, a former student of these schools, who was so torn between his Indian and white American identity that he gave in to the struggle and killed himself. According to Kelly, this was not an unusual event.

In 1969 a congressional report declared American Indian education "a national tragedy" and, gradually, government and church policy have shifted away from assimilation and the deplorable dehumanization of Native Americans. But the hurt and confusion of those earlier experiences, coupled with pockets of continuing prejudice, still take a shameful toll on the hearts and spirits of these American people.

Fog on Turtle Mountain

Born where sands boil and spew a hot fog
over blue prairie skies
and hide Turtle Mountain from view,
the woman with high, rippled-leather cheeks
stands in a schoolhouse door
moving between past and present
in a haunted dance
of old humiliation and new hope.

The children scurry by her,
red-brown skin aglisten with the sweat of play.
English flows with ease
from their Chippewa lips,
and they do not know the price they have paid,
nor that the woman framed in the door
forms a portrait of their past—
a light and dark contrast
with their hopeful youth,
her own childhood surrendered to the White Man's way.

Old memories stalk her like demented braves,
confusing the scene before her:
the motherless years at the mission school,
punctuated by the sting of coat hangers on her back
as she cried out in grief and loss;
the taste of brown soap in her mouth
as they tried to wash away
the language of her home.

But now she smiles at long black hair
that flies behind bronzed heads,
at "Hai", called out easily;
"Too bad" indeed, but no more with fear;
She shifts from her watch at the door,
steps into the western sunlight,
and gazes toward Turtle Mountain,
its gold-etched crest emerging cautiously
from hazy skies.

—1999

Where Joy Does Not Abide

In the rash of school killings during recent years, when children have murdered classmates and teachers, literally thousands of friends, family, and community members have been deeply and permanently affected. Sorrow, hate and despair abound in the families of both the victims and the children who kill. Christmas reminds us that the light, peace and joy of this season may not be enjoyed by those made sorrowful by these terrible events.

Where Joy Does Not Abide

Somewhere this Christmas night
There is a place where joy does not abide.
For out there somewhere
On this night of the Christ-child's birth
Is a place where another boy in loneliness
Waits on fate and ponders the emptiness
He thought his lethal acts would fill.
As faces of dying classmates and teachers
Parade in somber rank across his mind,
The proud revenge he felt at first
Is replaced by the starkness of truth.

Caroling Christmas bells
Ring in his ears
The discordant memories
Of death.

Yes, somewhere this Christmas night
There is a place where joy does not abide;
Where the peal of laughter
Mocks hopeless lives,
Robbed and pillaged and torn.
Somewhere there is a home where guilt and doubt
Fill hearts where peace and love should dwell;
And homes where childish merrymaking exists no more
And sadness stakes its claim.

Caroling Christmas bells
Toll through the night
The terrible memory
Of loss.

Somewhere on this sacred night
There is a place where joy does not abide,
Where flames of faith in the Holy Child
Waver and flicker in the winds of doubt;
Where the promises of Bethlehem
Fall cold on bruised and injured hearts,
And eyes are turned
From a distant star.

—1998

Where Are the Promises of Christmas?

I believe that anyone who has been in the presence of a child with a disability for long has most likely been joyfully surprised at the sheer courage and adaptability shown by that young person.

Christmas, with all of its visual beauty, had been for me, since the birth of my blind granddaughter, tinged with a certain sorrow and doubt. I wondered how this beloved child could claim the promises of the holy advent season. As I began to write this poem, I started to reflect on her spirit of determination to use the gifts and talents that she has been given. I realized with some surprise that she has indeed been able to capture the blessings of Christmas in a different, but possibly more meaningful, way than those of us who have sight.

Where Are the Promises of Christmas?

While choirs at Christmas sang the songs
Of light and hope and love,
And men of cloth from lofty stage
Proclaimed a God above
Who offered joy and peace to all
Who claimed Him as their Lord,
My heart in quiet derision
Rejected this cruel word.

I thought of her, that gentle child,
Who from birth had no sight,
Who never saw her mother's face,
And wondered, "Where is Light?"
But then her laughter pierced my thoughts
And lifted up my heart,
Reminding me that faith, and
Even light, in darkness start.

Her mother, in those blackest days,
Lent purpose to her life;
Through books and play and knowledge
They denied the way of strife.
She learned of hope and courage
And a God that made her whole;
And though her mother's face
She could not see, she saw her soul.

I pondered hope and thought of her

Whose future was unsure;
Obstacles would bar her way,
Her blindness had no cure.
Then I recalled how competent,
Determined, unafraid,
This child with brilliant spirit
Her gifts of God displayed.

And through my mind her music rang
From ivory keys she played;
Her voice sang out of Peace on Earth
And hope and love conveyed.
She'd walked her years with confidence,
With countless crises coped;
I knew that Someone held her hand
And clothed her life with hope.

Could there be love and hope and light
For such a child as she?
Was there a God of Christmastime
Who'd give her joy and peace?
As I reflected on her life
And how she'd touched my own,
And how, confronting handicap,
The seeds of hope she'd sown,

I understood from deep within
The grief was really mine,
That doubts and refutation
Had not her hopes maligned.
For through the beauty, love and grace
She'd scattered on her way,
God's promised gifts of Christmastime
Were hers this Christmas Day.
                              —December 1997

The Day the Bones Are Found

There is surely no agony and sorrow greater for parents than to experience the abduction of a child. Some cases are solved quickly, too often with the discovery that the child was murdered. This rapid and terrible conclusion leaves families in shock and grief. For others, the wait is long and torturous. "The families of missing children spend their lives in a kind of suspension, their imaginations pushing them toward dark conclusions." (Dan Reed, *Knight Ridder Newspapers*, February 1, 1999)

One mother of a child missing for ten years says that every time bones are found anywhere, she wonders if it is her child. For those who wait and wonder, life is lived in a distressing tension between hope that the child will someday come home and the horrible realization that the worst has happened and closure must be made.

The Day the Bones Are Found

There is a strange mixture
Of terror and hope
The day the bones are found
In a field near Monterrey.

In uncertain anticipation
The couple hover near the phone
And wonder if this will be the end
Of both hope and tortured wait.

The endless searching, searching
For the vanished child;
The calls that quicken their hearts
And assail their spirits.

The anguish of a fractured family
Held too long in captive grief;
A child's room enshrined like
A tomb juxtaposed to the living.

The years of wakeful nights,
The heart-gripping night fear,
The secret, guilty hope
That she is dead and not in pain.

And yet, the waning dream
That somehow, one day,
She will walk through the door,
Gives them life.

So they wait, not knowing
What to hope,
The day the bones are found
In a field near Monterrey.

—1999

65

Treachery

I have read with horror the news accounts of children abused by parents and caretakers. But I have always felt that death at the hands of one's mother must be, for a child, the ultimate treachery.

Treachery

I walk among the deep-etched dingy stones
That stand in somber contrast to
The stark white monument at his head.
They encircle him as if to shelter,
But, like me, they are too late.
Their inscriptions tell also of lives
That contrast with his—
Long years, dreams fulfilled, loving kin...

I know him only from stories I read and despise.
I come here now because my mother's heart
Will not believe;
But the clean white stone speaks a dirty truth—
A child lies beneath—
A child who knew and lived the dreadful tale I've read.
Now I stay and weep for children everywhere
Who know this unspeakable deed.

I kneel to trace his name with my fingers
As if to trace his short life
To this vile, untimely end,
And I notice an empty plot next to his
With a stone that bears no inscription but "Mother".
My breathing stops,
And my wounded heart wonders
If someday her ultimate treachery
Will be written there.

—1998

Mystery Solved

I recently witnessed a scene in a department store, which caused me to think about the aggression that children often exhibit in their behavior. A tall, strong, red-faced man at a checkout counter spoke to his wife and three little boys in words and tone that humiliated and embarrassed not only his family, but everyone in earshot. I went away pondering how it must be to live in a household where anger is apparently such a dominant force. While I do not mean to imply that all acts of aggression can always be so easily explained, I must pose the possibility that anger at society begins with anger in the home.

Mystery Solved

When you see
A sad-eyed child
In a public place
Being yanked around
By an angry adult
Who speaks
With wilting words,
Do you
Still wonder why
School grades are failed,
Buildings are vandalized,
And children shoot children?

—1999

Solution

The disruptive behavior of a child at school is often attributed to a bad attitude or lack of respect. However, as is revealed in this story told to me by a friend and elementary school counselor, a little one's troublesome actions can mask a far deeper and more distressing reason.

Solution

The door is closed
Against the school day din;
Counselor and child,
Like judge and defendant,
Sit face to face.
Recrimination and concern mingle
In uneasy alliance in her eyes;
In his, defiance holds its ground.

Tell me why, she says,
And recalls his crimes of the day;
His silence complicates her gruffness;
His sobs surprise her;
My mama's in jail, he says,
And if I be bad,
Maybe they'll put me in there, too.

In transforming mother-grace
She gathers the small boy to her,
In an embrace of collaborative grief.

—2000

About the Author

Johnnye Jo Lott is a former teacher who presently lives in North Carolina. A native of Natchitoches, Louisiana, Mrs. Lott is a graduate of Northwestern State University, Natchitoches, Louisiana, and has done graduate work in Georgia. Having earned four teaching certifications, she taught for eighteen years in public schools in New Orleans, Louisiana; Forsyth, Georgia; and

Johnnye Jo Lott

Alexandria, Louisiana. For nine years before moving to North Carolina, she owned and operated a Sylvan Learning Center. In North Carolina, she has found time to pursue her love of writing.

It was from her extensive experience with children of all ages, socio-economic levels and life situations— and her passion about the plights of these children— that Mrs. Lott wrote this collection of poems and narratives. *In the Cold of the Sun* is her first book.

She moved to Murfreesboro, North Carolina, in 1996, and lives there with her husband, Stan. They have three grown children and three grandchildren.